I Do... Over?

A Christian's Guide to Remarriage

Loraine D. Nunley

Copyright ©2012 Loraine D. Nunley

ISBN-13: 978-1479282951
ISBN-10: 1479282952

Cover Photo: CanStockPhoto.com/Anke/

All Rights Reserved.

No part of this book may be reproduced, stored in a retrieval system, or transmitted, in any form or by any means, electronic, mechanical, photocopying, recording, or otherwise, without the expressed written, dated and signed permission from the author.

Disclaimer

This book is intended to help remarried couples build a successful remarriage. Every attempt has been made to provide accurate, up to date and reliable complete information. This book and its author makes no guarantees of success as the strategies detailed in this book are dependent upon the individual work of the reader. Readers acknowledge that the author is not engaging in rendering legal, financial, medical or professional advice.

By reading this book, the reader agrees that under no circumstances is the author responsible for any losses, direct or indirect, which are incurred as a result of use of the information contained within this book, including – but not limited to errors, omissions, or inaccuracies.

All company names and websites are given by way of information and the author disclaims any and all responsibility for the content of external sites, your usage of those sites, and the accuracy of the information in them. *I Do...Over? A Christian's Guide to Remarriage* was not prepared, approved, licensed, sponsored, endorsed, associated with or affiliated with any of those companies.

Acknowledgements

To My Darling Thom – Who Knew?

Chapter One
In The Beginning

MISSION

Our mission is to show God's glory in the successfulness of our marriage despite overwhelming odds. We want to give hope and encouragement to others that remarriage can be successful through God. We want to educate people on how to help God make beauty from the ashes of failed marriages.

WHO ARE WE?

Thom and I will celebrate our tenth anniversary on October 24, 2012. We have a blended family (his, hers and ours). Our children range in age from six to nineteen.

My first marriage was for nine years to my high school sweetheart. Two of our older children are from that marriage. Our marriage is my second one. Thom's first marriage was for two years and our oldest child is from that marriage. His second marriage was for one year and there were no children from it. Our marriage is his third one. Our two oldest children have lived with their other parents (our ex-spouses) since they entered high school.

We married when our oldest children were ages six through nine and we each had sole physical custody of them with our spouses retaining joint legal custody and visitation rights. We lived within an hour from my ex, so my children spent every other weekend with their father and we split holidays. Thom's ex lived several states away so his child connected with his mother mostly via telephone. Our youngest children came along two years into our marriage.

HOW DID WE GET TO THIS PLACE?

It was our second month in the trailer - a 28-foot triple bunk travel trailer. We were waiting for the construction to be completed on our new home. Thom and I, along with the five children, who were six months to twelve years old at the time, were crowded into this confined space trying not to kill each other (a testament to God's grace for sure). It was at that time that Thom and I, both separately and together, cried out to God. "God, why?", "God, what are we to do?", "God, what is your will in all this?", and "God, what are we supposed to learn from this?" It was also at this time when we really held God to His promise that He would carry us through the fires (Isaiah 43:2). To say that this time frame was a low point in our marriage would be an understatement. It was at this time of trial that we not only found ourselves to be stronger than we ever knew we could be, but that we also sought some purpose for our trials. We began to look at our trials from the perspective of what we could learn from them and what knowledge we could possibly impart to others. We were cheated and treated wrongly by people. We had made some bad decisions and learned some hard lessons. There were so many things that we wanted to share with others. How could we narrow the field down so that we could really help someone? So then we asked ourselves this question: "What was the most important thing that happened to us?" And the answer was - US. There were lots of lessons we had learned, but nothing came close to the wonders that God had worked in our relationship.

As you read about our experiences and the glory of God's work through our relationship, we pray that God will use it to breathe life into your relationship with each other and with Him.

Chapter Two
Just the Facts

WHAT QUALIFIES OUR MARRIAGE AS A SUCCESS?

So now you want to know what our credentials are. Do we have a PhD in Psychology or a Doctorate in Marital Counseling? No. As a matter of fact, our formal education, which is accounting and engineering, have nothing to do with psychology, theology or any other "ologies". We are just graduates from the school of hard knocks. More accurately, we are lifetime students of God's school for the not perfect, yet forgiven. We have a love in our hearts for our Lord, Jesus Christ and a desire to help our fellow brothers and sisters in Christ to be successful in their marriages.

REMARRIAGE STATISTICS

Here are the facts surrounding our marriage:

- We have been married for 9 years and together for 10 years. We are more in love with each other today than we were yesterday. Today, our marriage is the strongest it has ever been and we have watched it grow stronger with each passing day.

- Our marriage is Thom's third marriage and he brought one child into our marriage.

- Our marriage is my second marriage and I brought two children into our marriage.
- Our marriage produced two children.

Now here are the statistics:

- The overall divorce rate for first marriages is 45-50% (U.S. Department of the Census, 2006).
- The divorce rate for second marriages is 60% and for third marriages is 73% (U.S. Department of the Census, 2006). It is assumed that successive marriages increase this percentage.
- Remarriage will occur for about 75% of those who divorce (U.S. Department of the Census, 2006).
- For stepfamilies where only one partner has brought in children, the divorce rate for remarriage climbs to 65% (Hetherington & Kelly, 2002).
- For stepfamilies where both partners bring in children, the rate climbs again to slightly more than 70% (Hetherington & Kelly, 2002).

There are no clear percentages for stepfamilies adding "our" children but the assumption is that this would increase the percentages as well.

We should also mention that these figures are from nationally represented sources. Since the government is not keeping clear data on remarriage, the estimates are possibly low. So let's add another 5% for that and the fact that we added "our" children to the mix, which brings the divorce rate for our marriage up to approximately 75% (conservatively speaking). As you can see, statistically speaking, we are a divorce waiting to happen.

STRESS STATISTICS

As if that weren't enough, let's add the STRESS factor into the mix.

Here is a list of the stressful life events that have occurred throughout the lifetime of our marriage (in no particular order):

- Self-employment
- Change in job multiple times
- Change from first shift job to second shift job
- Income change from two incomes to one
- Loss of job and primary income resulting in a substantial amount of time on unemployment
- Major fallouts with family members
- Parent's remarriage
- Change of residence seven times including a large move to a different state
- Change of school for children multiple times
- Homeschooling of children
- Military deployment during both war and peace times
- Child diagnosed with health issues
- Multiple high risk pregnancies

- Multiple high risk births
- Sterilization
- Death of four close family members
- Relocation of close family member
- Home foreclosure
- Home construction
- Living in a travel trailer for four months
- Bankruptcy
- Retirement from the military
- Going back to college full-time at forty years old
- Children going to live full time with other biological parent (one out of state)

According to the **Holmes Rahe Scale** (Holmes and Rahe Stress Scale, 2012) which measures life stress and your susceptibility to stress-induced health breakdown, if you have 300 points or more in a single year, there is an 80% chance that you will have a major health breakdown within two years. We scored over 300 points for eight years of our marriage. The large majority of this list probably occurred during the first half of our marriage. In addition to that, we need to keep in mind that we were experiencing stress from the residual effects of our divorces and the blending of our families at the same time. We are happy to report that we have not experienced any major health breakdowns.

Imagine what a 75% chance of divorce and an 80% chance of a major health breakdown would do to any marriage. It is safe to say that we have been through the fire and have survived. But more importantly, we have thrived and become successful where others have become ashes.

So what is our secret? Well, it's not really a secret or even a magic formula. Marriage is hard work – any meaningful relationship is. We've worked hard at making our marriage successful. We've already been through ones that have failed. What we can offer to you is HOPE. It can be done. You can beat those statistics! We offer you our *experiences* in what we have done that works. Will it work for you? Yes, most of the basics will. But there are never easy answers when it comes to people. You and your spouse are human beings with different personalities. That is where the work comes in. Are you willing to learn about each other and work at making your individual and uniquely special relationship last? If so, then follow us through our continuing journey to make our "do-over" a success!

Chapter Three
Unpack The Bags

WHAT MAKES REMARRIAGE DIFFERENT FROM A FIRST MARRIAGE?

The biggest problem within remarriage and the one thing that makes our marriages stand apart from first marriages can be summed up in one word – BAGGAGE. That is not to say that people do not bring baggage into a first marriage, but there are many first marriages that have little or no baggage. Maybe they brought a tote bag. In remarriage, we not only bring along a suitcase, but it seems as if we bring the whole moving truck with us. Remarriages *always* have baggage. There is no question about that because at the heart of the "re" marriage is a prior one. No matter how long or how short, good or bad that first marriage was, it has created baggage that you cannot discard. It's just a fact. Unfortunately, we go from bringing a lot of baggage into the marriage to setting it down in the middle of our living room and it becomes the big white elephant that we ignore. It is time to unpack the bags!!

GRIEVE.

In Isaiah 61:3, the Bible says that, for those that mourn, God will give them beauty for ashes and the oil of joy for mourning. God does this for the trials in our lives. Our marriage followed a fire and a death of sorts – the fiery crash and tragic deaths of our previous marriages. Mourn the death of your former marriages. How can you move on if you don't? Any grief counselor will tell you that you must grieve a death, so why should the death of a marriage be any different? This is part of the healing process.

How you grieve will be dependent upon your individual personalities because everyone handles death differently. The important thing is that you do recognize it as a death and that you *do* grieve. For me, time was a big help - time to myself to think about it and time in respect to distance from the actual divorce. If you jumped into a remarriage without grieving the first one, then do it now. It is okay to feel badly about the death of your prior marriage. It is also okay to grieve it and then move on.

LEARN FROM YOUR MISTAKES.

This is so very important for a remarriage. Like it or not, we made mistakes in our previous marriages. Don't put all the blame on other people. You must take responsibility for those mistakes that you were at fault for or that you facilitated. You can think of it as a very painful learning lesson, but a learning lesson none the less. When you apply what you have learned, you have become a better person. Our trials build our character. Does God want one of our trials to be divorce? No, of course not, but He will use it. The lemonade from the lemons we supply Him. At this point you can be thankful that you can begin again. This is your do-over. Let's take the example of communication, for instance. There are many new couples in first marriages that struggle with communication and they head down the path of divorce before they even identify the problem. Maybe some of you did that in your previous marriages. You now have an advantage – you already know that communication is something that needs to be worked on. Maybe you learned the hard way how to do it (or how not to do it). And not only can you make beauty from the ashes of a previous marriage, but you are now in the position to share these experiences with others like we are doing. God has now given you a ministry. Take that lemonade and share God's lemonade recipe with others.

ACKNOWLEDGE THE BAGGAGE - COMMUNICATION

Talk about your baggage with each other. Do not let there be any skeletons in the closet because you don't know if someday the maid (or somebody worse) will decide to clean out your closet. Secrets shared are no longer a threat to you after you share them. How can you talk about your past without that becoming a problem? Well, first of all, it is a bit of a dance, isn't it? The best way that we can tell anyone to go about it is in the fashion that we did. First of all, we let God speak for us. Discussing your past is not for you to air your dirty laundry to your new spouse. Some things are best left in the past. What we mean is a more general discussion about your past relationships – what worked, what didn't, how you found yourself responding to circumstances, what you learned and how it shaped the person you are now. You need to be honest, but not brutally so. There isn't really any need to name names or give intimate details. The purpose is for you to clear the air and to get a deeper understanding of each other. The best rule of thumb is that you should only say those things that either help your relationship or protect it. If what you say doesn't do one or both of these things, then you probably shouldn't say it. If you are unsure as to how to do this without crossing a line of hurt or anger, then talk to a counselor or a mentor first. This is why we say that you need to let God guide your conversations, because He will let you know what you should reveal and what you should not. Our relationship was built on many long conversations with each other about such things. It has helped us to understand our spouse in many meaningful ways. God has also used those revelations to protect us from outside attacks. This example is an illustration. When we were first engaged, we had some family members that were against it. In a heated disagreement over the subject, a family member threatened us with revealing a secret to the other in an attempt to "blackmail" us into postponing our wedding. As we had already disclosed the "secret", the threat had no effect on us. In fact, we were completely surprised that this person would stoop to such an act. This just goes to show you that you never know what Satan will use to destroy that which glorifies God.

HOW DO YOU MAKE EACH OTHER FEEL?

Look at your spouse. This is the most important person in your life now. This is your best friend. The other piece of your heart. Treasure each other. Make each other feel like the king or queen of your life. The death of a marriage is a direct hit to our self-esteem, no matter who is at fault. Because of that, most of us are extremely sensitive and vulnerable to the way a new spouse treats us. Things that may not have been a big deal in a first marriage can become the biggest arguments in a remarriage. Comparison is one of those things. It seems to be a part of human nature to compare people to other people. Even in the bible,

Jesus has to rebuke Peter for comparing himself to John (John 21:20-22). In remarriage, there is a previous spouse to compare the current one to. No one likes to be compared in a negative fashion to someone else, particularly someone that held your affections for any length of time. Even comparison in a positive fashion can be problematic because the comparison shows that your thoughts are on the other person. Because no one is perfect, except for Jesus, we must work at keeping our comparisons to a minimum and to ourselves most of the time. It is very difficult to build upon a relationship that has someone else coming in between (even if it is only in your thoughts). For those with stepchildren, comparison to a former spouse can not only be a problem, it can be deadly in a remarriage. This is because there is still contact with the previous spouse. Also, stepchildren are experts at the comparison game.

THE GRASS IS GREENER - GRATITUDE.

Don't make the mistake of falling into the "grass is greener" syndrome. Someone once said that the grass isn't greener on the other side, there's just more fertilizer over there. You need to seed and water your own grass. If you do, you will find that the grass is always greener right where you are at.

Lack of gratitude is probably at the heart of most relationship problems. It is difficult to be unhappy in a relationship when you are grateful to have it in the first place. Remarried couples should have an easier time being grateful for their remarriage because they have a failed marriage behind them. Ironically, we do not seem to have an easier time with it. Perhaps it is just human nature to be more aware of what others have that we don't. Perhaps we are afraid to embrace our remarriages because of our past failures. What matters is that we do something about it. Our marriage is much stronger than our previous marriages were and we are grateful every day for that. The stronger our marriage is, the further we move away from those doom and gloom statistics that our "do-over" will not last. Make it your goal to have your grass be the greenest in the neighborhood!

Chapter Four
God is First Priority

HOW HAVE WE ATTAINED A SUCCESSFUL MARRIAGE?

We have a secret. It's not a huge secret, but it is one of those secrets that most people just look over because they don't want that to be the solution. Here's the secret... Are you ready for this? One word. The secret is GOD. God as in Jehovah Jireh, Yahweh, Jesus Christ in the flesh. Not <u>A</u> God, but <u>THE</u> God. The God who created this beautiful planet in six days (Genesis 1-2). The God who knew us and knit us together in our mother's womb (Psalm 139:13). The God who became flesh in the form of Jesus Christ, walked among us, died for our sins and rose again triumphing over death (Book of John). The God who wants a personal relationship with each and every one of us. He is the secret. Or more accurately, the KEY. What is your relationship like with your creator? God must be the #1 priority in your marriage. He must be the cornerstone. He created marriage and it is His design. Who better to have as your foundation than the one who created it?

Our previous marriages did not have God as a major player. We were fortunate to come to that realization before we were even put together. I came to a place where I determined, in my heart, that God would be the number one priority in my life and if that meant that I would be divorced and single for the rest of my life here on earth, I was willing to do that. God had spent too much time on the back burner. And as God's timing is always perfect, Thom had come to the same state of heart around the same time. It was at this determination that God was finally able to put us into each other's lives. During this time, I was keeping a prayer journal. As I read back over my emotions and feelings during this time and during the months of our courtship, I can see the recurring theme of asking God to make sure that I kept that promise to Him. You must make it your mission to put God first in everything. This requires work because as humans, we are naturally self-centered. It is sometimes hard to pull yourself out of your own world to put God back in charge of it. And He must be in charge of your marriage. What a comfort to me to know that I could rely upon Him to take care of it. So God must be first for both of you.

We make a conscious effort to encourage each other in our individual relationships with God and we make a conscious effort to place God into our collective relationship. The important thing to remember is that God must come first with each of you individually and with you as a couple. This is done in a few ways.

Prayer

As with any good relationship, you must communicate with one another. Prayer is one of the most powerful and direct ways to communicate with God. You should encourage each other in your prayer lives. As an example, if one of us is having a bad day, many times the other will ask if we've prayed or talked to God about it. Sometimes in the midst of our trials, we forget that God is the first place we should turn to. We remind each other that He is there. The beautiful part of being in a marriage relationship is that you can strengthen each other. When one is down, the other can lift up and vice versa.

Not only is it important to pray individually, but it is equally important for us to pray as a couple. Matthew 18:20 (NKJV) says "For where two or three are gathered together in My name, I am there in the midst of them." Your marriage meets those criteria. If you and your spouse are praying together, God will be there in a powerful way. We have also found that it encourages us to hear our spouse in prayer. We are encouraged by their heart speaking to God, we are encouraged by their words on our behalf, and we are encouraged by the love and support that shows itself during these moments in communication with our God. Due to the number of emotions that arise when we are praying, we experience a new level of intimacy together.

Reading the Bible

The Bible is God's love letter to His children. There is no better place to learn about God and become closer to Him than through His Word. Certainly you should deepen your individual relationship with God by reading the Bible. But as with prayer, there are benefits to reading the Bible as a couple. The Bible is the most wonderful *living* book. You can read through it over and over again and you will never get everything there is to know out of it. That makes it like opening a present, because you can gain some new knowledge or insight every time you read it. If that can happen to you individually, think about what can happen if the two of you are reading as a couple. With different personalities and perspectives, we find even more insights. Our pastor can preach on a passage of scripture that we have heard or even read ourselves many times and we can still get new insights from his perspective.

We highly recommend reading *Song of Solomon* together. Read it to each other and mean it. What a boost to a husband's ego when his wife reads to him things like Song of Solomon 1:16 (NKJV), *Behold, you are handsome, my beloved! Yes, pleasant!* What wife wouldn't love to hear her husband read Song of Solomon 4:9 (ESV), *You have captivated my heart, my sister, my bride; You have captivated my heart with one glance of your eyes, with one jewel of your necklace.*

Worship

You will find that many of the things that you should be doing personally with your relationship with God, you should also be doing as a couple. Worship is one of those things. Why? Because the heart of worship is placing God at the very center of things and that is something which you need to do both personally and as a couple. The dictionary defines worship in the verb form as "extravagant respect or admiration for or devotion to an object of esteem". God created humans as creatures of worship. We must worship something. The Bible is clear that we are to worship God. Deuteronomy 5:7 (NIV) says, "You shall have no other gods before Me." The Psalms are filled with verses on worshiping our God for who He is. Not only is it very important and an act of obedience to worship your creator, but the act of worshiping together as a couple serves to bring you even closer together as a unit. Music is a powerful thing. It is capable of creating enormous emotions in a person. Couple that with music and song directed to our God and the emotions can be off the charts! Those emotions for God also magnify the depth of your feelings for each other. You don't have to even be aware of your spouse's voice or the words they are singing, humming or playing. The focus of worship is on God. But the residual benefits to your marriage can be astounding.

Discussion

Both of us are thinkers and talkers. This makes for many conversations and discussions. Add our favorite topic – Jesus, and you have a recipe for some great bonding conversations. Talking about God helps us to grow. We learn from each other's experiences and perspectives. Talking about God also helps us to stay connected to Him. We hardly have time to sin if God is at the forefront of our thoughts through our discussions. Of course, the idea here is to discuss God, not just talk *at* each other. Now you and/or your spouse may not be talkers but this is something that you should work on because talking is a form of communication and communication is a must in any successful relationship.

Submission to God

We must stress here that much of our success comes from simple obedience and submission to God and His authority. As God was not a major player in our former marriages, obedience to Him was also not a major consideration for us. Looking back, we can see those times when we would shy away from God and any feelings of remorse over our disobedience, and we can see the many justifications that we gave to ourselves and others for it. Suffice it to say, we have learned the hard way, that God's ways are the best and that our obedience and submission are for our good in the same way that our children's obedience and submission to us is good for them. If you look through the Bible, you will see many examples of God having to punish his children for disobedience, convict them for not submitting to His authority or just let them face the consequences of the paths they chose for themselves. Much of our problems in our former marriages, and the ones that we learned the most from, were brought on by our insistence that we knew more than God did about what was best for us. Are we still disobedient to Him? Do we still struggle with submission to His will? Of course, we wouldn't be human unless we did. But within our marriage, we have learned to recognize it quicker and fix it. It is not easy sometimes, but as our success shows, it is definitely worth it.

Chapter Five
We Are Each Other's Priority

RELATIONSHIP TO EACH OTHER

If our greatest ingredient of success for our remarriage is the relationship we have with God, our second greatest ingredient is the relationship that we have with each other. If you are saying to yourselves, "This sounds like it could apply to any marriage, not just remarriage," you would be correct. We will address the specific areas that make remarriages different, but keep in mind that many of the keys to success in marriage are the same whether this is your first or your fifth.

Priority

Your spouse must be the priority of your earthly relationships. Your spouse only comes second to God. The Bible is very clear on this. Genesis 2:24 (NIV) says, "That is why a man leaves his father and mother and is united to his wife, and they become one flesh." ONE flesh – how's that for priority? For obvious reasons, your flesh is your priority much of the time, even without being conscious of it. You breathe automatically. You have needs for sustenance and rest. So if you are to be one flesh with your spouse, doesn't that indicate that your spouse should be as important to you as your own flesh?

Now, we are not suggesting that this is easy. In our busy lives, we often try to put our bodies lower on the priority list. If we have trouble with those things that are a necessity to our own bodies, how much more so will we have trouble with the rest? No, this is by no means easy. But as we stated earlier, any good relationship requires work. And this is one of those areas. It is especially hard when you have children. But God expects it and we can tell you that when you follow God's plan – it works. And don't forget the other side of the equation – just as you are to make your spouse your priority only after God, so your spouse must make you their priority as well. This is where things balance out.

So how do you do it? Life has to go on, right? You cannot spend all of your waking moments catering to your spouse, can you? No, of course not. And God doesn't want it that way. If He did, there would be no instructions on the different roles that we must play as parents, or friends to others. So there must be a balance there. Does your spouse know that if they needed you, you would drop everything for them? Does your spouse know that even when you are not with them physically, you are there emotionally and spiritually? Can they be confident that they are on your mind (in a good way) much of the time? And do you know those same things yourself?

It is always funny to us how often we are on each other's minds. God has a way of putting the thoughts there just when we need them. We have lost track of the number of times that we have picked up the phone to call the other and have them say, "I was just thinking about you."

Commitment

Making each other the priority in your lives is a commitment and part of the biggest commitment you make in a marriage. This is very important. In our previous marriages, we lost that commitment. We don't want to make that mistake again. We have to be committed to God, to this marriage and to each other. This commitment stems from a determination to work at this relationship without giving up. We have determined that this will be our last marriage while we are here on earth together. One thing that we have learned from our previous marriages is that the "D" word (Divorce) should not be part of our vocabulary. We don't talk about it as an option, we don't think about it as an option. As far as we are concerned, it is not an option. The only way out of this marriage is death or rapture. Preferably rapture.

Compromise

Every good relationship must have compromises. Every good marriage must have them. But it is especially important to have compromise in a remarriage. This isn't a clean slate. There is a lot of baggage with remarriage. Compromise is even more a player in a blended family remarriage. You have your own ideas, experiences (good or bad), traditions and expectations and your spouse has their own. This is a give and take. Make sure that you are doing both. If one of you is the giver and one of you is the taker, the marriage will be off balance. Like riding a seesaw, if you are off balance, the ride just isn't as much fun. And the ability to go higher together is greater with more balance.

Communication

This brings us to the important matter of communication. Compromise will only come with good communication. Again, for as important as communication is in a normal marriage and relationship, it is even more important in a remarriage. Talk to each other. Talk about what you want your relationship to be. Talk about what God has called you to be as a couple. Did we think that God was calling us to this ministry when He put us together? No. Sometimes it was a struggle just to get up and keep moving every day. But we did know that God had something in mind for us. Even from the beginning. Those ideas and dreams fuelled us. We have spent many hours contemplating how God was working in our lives and what He has in store for us. Just as it is so important to keep the lines of communication open with God, so it is important to keep the lines open with your spouse.

We have built a relationship around absence of fear or embarrassment. Almost everything we say to each other is out of our love for each other (love which is strengthened by God's love and priority in our marriage).

In a remarriage, there are times when you can feel, or make your spouse feel, like you are walking into the middle of a play. The cast has already been set and introduced. The play has begun and you are trying to figure out the plot. Hence, the need for communication. Again we say: Talk to each other. Clue your spouse in on what act your play is in. Give the stage whisper with the directions so that they know how their part is to play out. Never assume that your spouse knows what you are thinking or that your spouse *should* know what you are thinking. Only God can read minds and even He requires that we talk to Him.

You are in this marriage for the duration. Never throw out the "D" word unless it is a factual reference to you having one in your past or talking about someone else's. Don't tease about it – don't threaten each other with it – don't even entertain thoughts about it. Our society has made divorce easy to use as a band-aid for marital unhappiness. You, more than most people, should understand the true consequences of that word and the damage it causes. This is your second chance to work within God's plan – Don't blow it!

Another aspect of communication that you need to work on with your spouse is non-verbal communication. There will be times when words cannot or even should not be used, but that doesn't mean that you cannot have good communication. The better you know your spouse and the better your relationship is, the better you will be at non-verbal communication. The more of your senses that you use in your relationship, the more you enhance it. Find out what non-verbal things enhance your relationship.

Love and Romance

If you love someone, it is important to show it. We have already talked about communication, but *telling* your spouse that you love them regularly is another aspect of communication that is revitalizing. Not too many people are turned off by hearing "I love you." We have found that the things we do to show our love for each other energizes us.

We have also found non-verbal, non-touching communication to be a good tool for providing strength to our relationship. A wink, a special wave, a certain look, etc – all of these things can be done at a distance to let your spouse know that you are thinking of them and that you care. Personally, we frequently make use of the sign language sign for "I love you". It is simple, can be done with one hand, and can be understood from quite a distance away. We use it like we would a wave, but it means much more.

Anything that utilizes our senses is a gift. Touching is a great example. You can save the intimate stuff for the privacy of your own bedroom or home, but affectionate touching in an appropriate manner is great. Something as simple as a man placing his hand on the small of his wife's back or a woman placing her hand on her husband's cheek can be very powerful in strengthening your marriage. The touch lets your spouse know that you are thinking about them. You should be in the habit of touching your spouse every day. A hug or kiss when you leave each other or when you see each other for the first time that day. A tender caress of the cheek or brush of the hair can be the difference between a good mood and a bad one. Take your spouse's hand when you are out in public walking. Touch their shoulder when you lean in to hear them or to look at something together. We have seen a gentle hand placed on top of the knee or across the back diffuse anger and tame a hurtful retort. The important thing is to let your spouse know, in a tangible way, that you are there for them and that you care.

Respect

The Bible tells us in Ephesians Chapter 5, verses 22-33, that husbands are to love their wives as Christ loves the church and that wives are to respect their husbands and be submissive to them as the church is to Christ. We recommend attending a "Love and Respect" conference. You can check out their ministry online (loveandrespect.com). It is a wonderful tool that teaches this and is great for strengthening your relationship. We attended one of these seminars when we were first married and then took the video seminar at our church a few years later. God is very deliberate in how He says that things should work. He created us, "man and woman", and He knows just how things should work for the maximum benefit of his creation. Now you would think that this would be common sense, wouldn't you? But we so often look to our own selfishness that we forget that the creator is much more capable, than we ever will be, at maximizing our potential. Here is one of those areas where we often find that we need reminding of how things work.

We talked about love earlier and now we are talking about respect. As God commands, women are to respect their husbands, but that is not to say that husbands do not have to respect their wives. One of the ways that we respect each other is through a respect of hierarchy. Webster's dictionary defines hierarchy as "a ruling body of clergy organized into orders and ranks each subordinate to the one above it or a body of persons in authority". Quite simply, this is the order of authority. Everyone has some form of authority over them. Our bosses, our government, and our law enforcement are some examples of that.

Well, our marriage and family work similarly. God is the head of the marriage, Man is the head of the woman and family, Parents are the heads of their children. This may sound old-fashioned, but we respect the hierarchy that God set up. God made man and woman very special and very different. He created us to fill different roles in the marriage. First of all, to mess with that is like telling God that He doesn't know what He is doing. Are you telling the inventor how His invention should work? (Remember the common sense?) Secondly, it works. Speaking from a woman's perspective and particularly my own experience when I was the head of my household as a single mother, I am quite content to hand that responsibility over to someone else. I did a pretty good job as the head of the household, but as a woman, I am not naturally good at it. I am also quite busy handling my role as a woman, which is time consuming in and of itself. Similarly, Thom has had some experience in trying to fill a mother's role for his son and be the head of his household at the same time. Again, it can be done, but it is in some respects like using a piece of string to replace a wire in a machine. It may work, but it is not the best way of doing things. The potential for breaking down is much greater when all of the parts are not able to do the jobs they were meant to do. Having a marriage that celebrates our individual roles as God meant them to be has caused us to look with compassion at all of those relationships that don't run that way. Our society has caused men to be devalued and women to be discontent with themselves.

Submission to your spouse

We recommend the "Love and Respect" materials to give you a clear view of submission. But as a note, many women feel that they lose themselves in the concept of being submissive. You do not. Not if it is done right. I am a very opinionated and open person with my husband. If I don't agree with something, I will speak up. Submission can be very difficult for me at times. However, it is a matter of obedience to what God commands and I have always come out ahead for having worked at it. As the author of this book with clear opinions, do I appear to be a woman that doesn't know my own mind? Do I appear to be a woman who has lost myself in submission to my husband? Perhaps it would surprise you to know that I have gained more strength from my submission. Also, some men feel that submission is an excuse for being a bully. Again, not a biblical concept. Men, a submissive wife is a treasure. Treat her like one. And don't forget that just as a wife is to be submissive to her husband, you likewise are to be submissive to God. Wow. Ladies, I think, in some respects, we have the easier road here.

Another aspect of respect in a marriage relationship is the respect of our personalities. What does that mean? It means understanding your spouse's personality and using it to benefit your marriage. Don't try to change your spouse's personality, after all, isn't that the personality that you agreed to marry in the first place? Use each other's personalities to strengthen your marriage. For example, Thom is outgoing and friendly, and I am on the shy side when meeting new people. When we are in a setting with new people, I rely on him to "break the ice" for me and he relies on me to "reign in him" if he is monopolizing the conversations. If not handled right, our personalities could be a detriment to a circumstance rather than a benefit.

Chapter Six
Apply What You Have Learned

DURING NORMALICY

Reminisce

One of the most important keys to the success of our marriage is something that came quite naturally to us. It was not something that we discussed; it was just something that came about. It wasn't until we were asking God what He was using to give us success that we discovered it. That key is reminiscing. If you are picturing an elderly couple sitting on their front porch rocking in their rocking chairs and saying to one another, "Why I remember when...", then you need to get rid of that picture right now. This key is so powerful that you should be taking advantage of it long before you run out of things to talk about.

Reminisce: the process or practice of thinking or telling about past experiences. Now we would like to adjust that definition a bit. Reminisce is the practice of telling about past *good* experiences. The idea of reminiscing is that you are bringing to mind good experiences and feelings. For example, we reminisce many times about how we first met-up with each other. We talk about every detail. We talk about the facts of the meeting, we talk about how we felt, and we talk about what we were thinking. This is a great memory for us.

The reason that reminiscing works is that you revive those good feelings about each other. You basically stoke the fires of your love. You remind each other why you fell in love. In the midst of reminders, how can you lose sight of it? Our children roll their eyes when we reminisce so we know it is working. Others may get tired of hearing it, but it never gets old with the ones reliving it.

Dreams

Another thing that can be successful in growing your remarriage is dreaming together. Dreams give us hope, stoke the fires of our creativity, give us ambition and smooth the edges of the harsh realities of life. Like reminiscing, dreaming creates good feelings between you. Dreams give your marriage common goals. They help your communication because you are discussing them with each other. They bring you closer together because you are sharing with each other. Dream big and dream small. Dream for the possible and for the impossible. The great thing about dreams is that they are fluid. They can change. What we dreamed together when we first were married has changed as our marriage grows. Some dreams have come to fruition. Some dreams have faded away as new dreams have taken their place. Work toward your shared dreams, but be flexible enough to keep dreaming and changing the dreams as your marriage grows.

Conflict Management

Managing conflict is important in any relationship, but with the amount of baggage that a remarriage brings, it is especially important. We have each learned some valuable lessons from our previous marriages that we have discussed and applied to our marriage. We have taken the time to get to know each other so well that we know what our "hot buttons" are and how our personalities need to be handled. Do we fight? Of course. In fact, Thom and I can fight with the best of them. We have even had a few arguments with raised voices. But we have learned how to fight effectively. For instance, we never resort to name calling no matter how mad we get. We make the effort to remind ourselves whenever we are mad at each other, that we love each other. We may be really mad at each other right now, but ultimately we love each other. And we know that our spouse loves us. Focusing on our love for each other and for God helps us to control how we respond in an argument. We will often state things in a way that projects how we are feeling rather than finger pointing. We tell each other how the other is making us feel by their actions. And that is an important thing. It is the actions that we are usually angry about. It is not the man, but the sin – have you heard that? While reminding ourselves that we love the man (or woman) – we separate them from the action. We can get mad about the action. We can change our actions but our feelings haven't changed.

Learning from our mistakes

Probably the most important thing in a remarriage is the ability to learn from our mistakes and apply what we have learned. It is the lack of this that is the driving force behind the increased failure of subsequent marriages. If you've heard the saying "Those who do not learn from history are doomed to repeat it," then you know what we are talking about. This sounds simple, but for the human race, it seems to be one of the hardest things we do. Perhaps our pride is the problem there. You have to admit you have made mistakes before you can learn from them. Don't let your pride stand in the way of your happiness, though. While it is not a pleasant process sometimes, it is definitely worth it. What did you do to contribute to the breakdown of your former marriage? And be honest about it. The breakdown of a marriage comes from both parties, even if one is more at fault than the other. You don't have to beat yourself up over your mistakes, just take them as a learning experience that strengthens your character. Apply what you have learned. You will make your life with your new spouse infinitely better by doing so.

Overall interaction

How you interact with each other normally will dictate how successful your remarriage will be. How do you talk to each other? How do you talk *about* each other? How do you make each other feel? Naturally the answers to those questions should be positive. Otherwise you may need some work. Do you build your spouse up? Do you offer positive comments to each other? Are you appreciative of the person your spouse is and what they do in your life? What about when your spouse is not around? Do you sing your spouses praises to your friends? Or do you bash them when they are not around? Unkind words about your spouse should never pass your lips, even in jest. Again, this goes back to what happens in your thought process. If you are talking positively about your spouse to someone else, you give little thought to anything negative and therefore you build your relationship. Also, your spouse can be secure that your love shows through to others. Do you make each other feel loved? Appreciated? Desired? Wanted? Handsome or beautiful? Like the most important person on earth? Like a treasure? No one likes to feel unloved, unappreciated, undesirable, unwanted, etc.

Remember that everything you do and say should be purposeful in building up your spouse and your relationship.

Your spouse is your best friend. If they are not your best friend here on earth, than you need to change things. This is the person that you share your life with. You share your family, you share your circumstances, and you share yourself physically and emotionally. You share your dreams with each other. Cultivate those things that bring you closer together. Maybe that is similar interests and hobbies. The more time you spend together, the more your relationship grows.

DURING STRESS.

The hardest thing to do during times of stress is the normal things. But it is those things that you need to work at when you are stressed. What do we do when stress occurs? We reminisce. We reinforce our love for each other both verbally and physically. We pray. We stay close to God so that He can carry us through. We laugh. Laughter is a great stress reliever and a great relationship builder. Remember that you and your spouse are in this life together. It is you against the world, not against each other. You must have a united front even with your children, especially with step-children. Step-children can and frequently will push the boundaries to create division. Often, particularly in a remarriage, we take a solo stance against everyone and put our spouse behind enemy lines. Don't do it. Whether subconsciously or deliberately, it is a mistake. When all is said and done, you made a covenant with the Lord to hold your spouse at the highest level only below God Himself. A marriage is a powerful thing when it is done God's way. Satan is looking to destroy anything that gives honor and glory to God and marriage does that. Look at our society today. Anti-marriage is being promoted and good marriage is being destroyed. Be intentional about what you want your remarriage to be and pursue that with all of your might.

Chapter Seven
When All is Said and Done

God is so wonderful and completely awesome. We spend so much of our time as humans, blaming Him for all of our shortcomings. We blame Him for all of our bad choices. We blame Him for other people's bad choices. It is never God's desire that we make bad choices, but He did give us free will to do so and He respects our wishes. We can turn away from bad choices, give him the lemons and He can make the most wonderful lemonade! God hates divorce (Malachi 2:16). Obviously He didn't want it to happen (the lemons). But we are a living testament to the fact that God can make remarriage a wonderful thing (the lemonade). We, in no way, endorse divorce. We wholeheartedly believe in the sanctity of marriage. But as you have seen from the statistics, divorce is a reoccurring event in our society. As such, there are many of you that find yourselves in our position. Thankfully, our God is a God of infinite forgiveness and healing. So we seek forgiveness for that part we have played in something that God hates and we seek His healing in our future relationships. Remarriage can be successful as long as God is allowed to be the healer. It is our heart's desire to see your remarriage grow and flourish as ours has done. And while we are at it, let's help others to strengthen their remarriages. And while we are reducing the divorce statistics for remarriage, we can reach out to first marriages and help them reduce theirs. Ultimately, it is our responsibility to work at our relationships and we hope that we have given you the tools to make your remarriage "do over" last!

Works Cited

Hetherington, E. M., & Kelly, J. (2002). *For Better or For Worse: Divorce Reconsidered.* New York: W.W. Norton & Company, Inc.

Holmes and Rahe Stress Scale. (2012, July 25). Retrieved from Wikipedia: http://en.wikipedia.org/wiki/Holmes and Rahe stress scale

U.S. Department of the Census. (2006). *Statistical Abstract of the United States (122nd ed.).* Washington DC: US Government Printing Office.

About the Author

Loraine Nunley and Thom, her husband of ten years, live in Texas with their three children and pets. She is an author, accountant and stay-at-home mom. Aside from writing, she enjoys spending time with her family and reading.

If you enjoyed and/or were helped by this book, please leave a review to let others know about it. You are also welcome to visit and leave comments at our website:
http://www.successfulchristianremarriage.com

Made in the USA
Charleston, SC
04 November 2012